EVEN REVOLUTIONARIES LIKE CHOCOLATE CHIP COOKIES

Selected cartoons from
STILL A FEW BUGS IN THE SYSTEM

Other Doonesbury books by G. B. Trudeau

THE PRESIDENT IS A LOT SMARTER
THAN YOU THINK

DON'T EVER CHANGE, BOOPSIE

EVEN REVOLUTIONARIES LIKE CHOCOLATE CHIP COOKIES

a Doonesbury book

By G. B. Trudeau

POPULAR LIBRARY • NEW YORK

POPULAR LIBRARY EDITION

Copyright © 1970, 1971, 1972 by G. B. Trudeau

Library of Congress Catalog Card Number: 70-182752

Reprinted by arrangement with
Holt, Rinehart and Winston, Inc.

The cartoons in this book have appeared in newspapers in the United States and abroad under the auspices of Universal Press Syndicate.

PRINTED IN THE UNITED STATES OF AMERICA

GOBBLE!!
GOBBLE, GOBBLE!
GOBBLE, GOBBLE!
HA! HA!
HA!
HA.
78
77
10

HA! HA!
GOBBLE! GOBBLE!
HA!
GOBBLE!
HA!
HA!
HA!
78
78
10
GBTrudeau

BOY, DO I HATE COLLEGE MIXERS! BOY, DID I HAVE A LOUSY TIME!

I ALWAYS HAVE A LOUSY TIME! I NEVER MEET ANY GIRL! HOW DID B.D. EVER TALK ME INTO GOING?!

I DIDN'T WANT TO GO, BUT MY ROOMMATE B.D. ASSURED ME THAT I'D HAVE A GOOD TIME....

I HATE MY ROOMMATE B.D.
GB Trudeau

O.K., LET'S HAVE A QUICK RUNDOWN OF THE NEW LINE THEY JUST PUT IN!
10
77
20
7

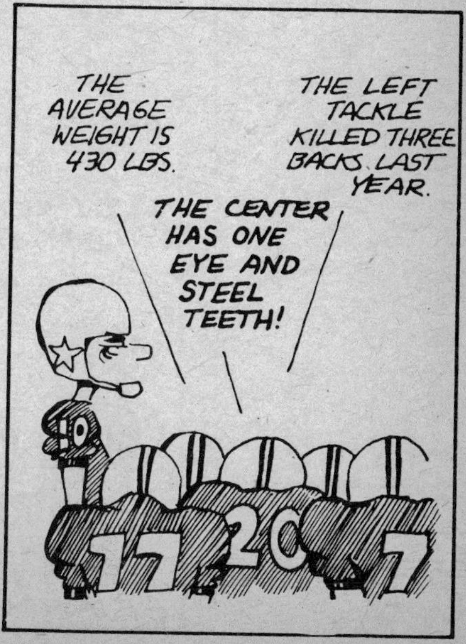
THE AVERAGE WEIGHT IS 430 LBS.
THE CENTER HAS ONE EYE AND STEEL TEETH!
THE LEFT TACKLE KILLED THREE BACKS LAST YEAR.
10
77
20
7

GBTrudeau

CATHY, I'M GLAD YOU COULD COME TODAY. I WANT TO GET YOUR REACTION TO A GUY CALLED SAM SMOOTH, WHO APPARENTLY GIVES LESSONS IN **ATTRACTING WOMEN**!!

FRANKLY, MIKE, I'VE NEVER HEARD OF ANYTHING SO AB....

HULLO, MY NAME'S SMOOTH. YOU MUST BE MIKE...

WHAT ARE
YOUR RATES,
SAM?

GBTrudeau

O.K., DOONESBURY, WATCH ME CAREFULLY... THIS IS LESSON #2 OF THE SAM SMOOTH METHOD OF ATTRACTING WOMEN!

EXCUSE ME, LUV, BUT HOW WOULD YOU LIKE TO GO OUT WI...
GASP...
AIIEE!!

HUM... A SMALL CROWD OF STUDENTS AND FACULTY HAS FORMED OUTSIDE.

THEY ARE PROBABLY ALL WONDERING, "WHO IS THIS BRAVE YOUNG MAN WHO HAS TAKEN OVER THE PRESIDENT'S HOUSE?"

WELL, THAT DOES IT!
I'VE FINALLY FINISHED
MY 30 PAGE TERM
PAPER ON FRANKLIN
ROOSEVELT...

R-R-R...

R-R-R-R...

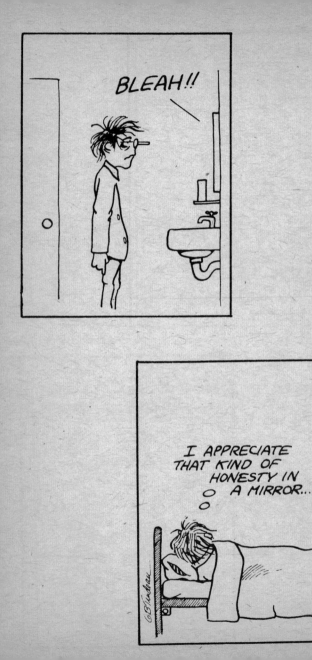

WELL, MIRROR! HOW ABOUT THAT, HUH? I'M GETTING TO BE QUITE A LOOKER, EH?
I'M NOT YOUR MIRROR. I'M YOUR PAUL NEUMAN POSTER.

HEY, MIRROR! DON'T FORGET TO MENTION THE YOU-KNOW-WHATS!

OH YES, MIKE, ABOUT YOUR COMPLEXION...
GBTrudeau

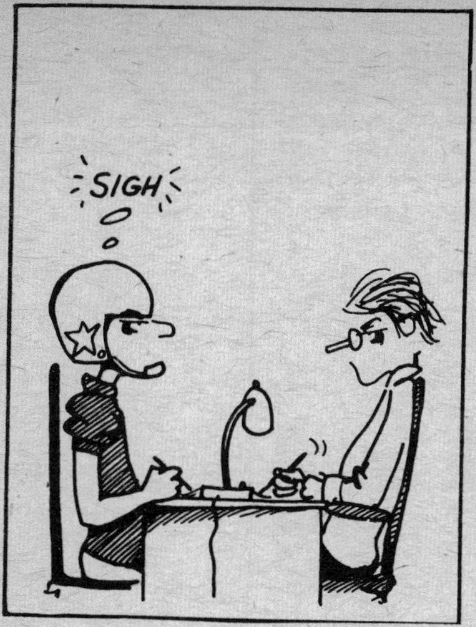
SIGH

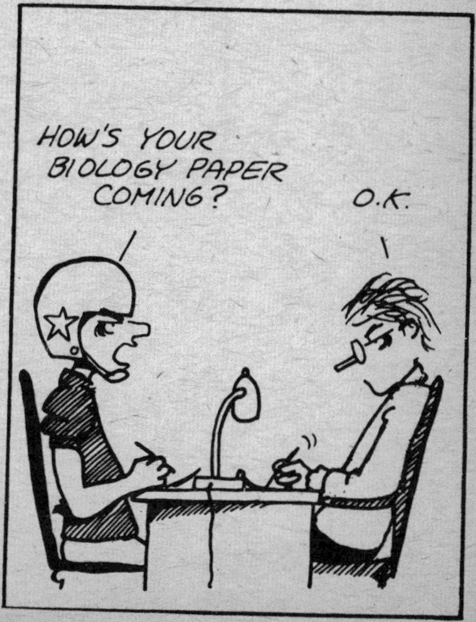
HOW'S YOUR BIOLOGY PAPER COMING?
O.K.

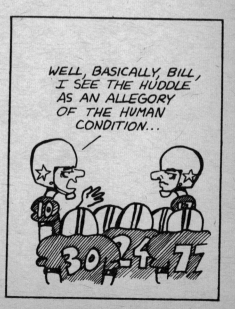

HOH, BOY, IT'S FOURTH AND TEN, AND I'VE FORGOTTEN WHAT PLAY TO CALL...

RATS! WHAT IS IT I'M SUPPOSED TO CALL?... IT'S BEEN SO LONG SINCE WE'VE HAD A FOURTH DOWN...

LILY, I THINK IT'S IMPORTANT THAT YOU UNDERSTAND I ONLY WANT A VERY CASUAL RELATIONSHIP, NOTHING SERIOUS...

SNIFF I'M SORRY TO HEAR THAT, MIKE... THAT BEING THE CASE, I WOULDN'T FEEL RIGHT ABOUT GOING OUT TO YOUR CAR...

YOU KNOW, LILY,
PERHAPS I'M BEING
TOO HASTY...

MARK, IF YOU WANT TO STAY HOME THIS VACATION, YOU'RE GOING TO HAVE TO GET YOUR HAIR CUT.

IS THAT YOU, MARK? DID YOU GET YOUR HAIR CUT AS PER MY INSTRUCTIONS?

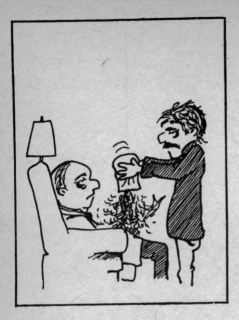

MERRY CHRISTMAS.

GBTrudeau

IT'S **CHRISTMAS EVE** AS
A TIRED, DISAPPOINTED,
AND DISILLUSIONED
STUDENT ACTIVIST
DROPS OFF TO SLEEP...

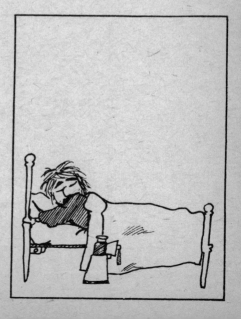

I THOUGHT I
HEARD REINDEER..

WHEE! IT'S ALMOST MIDNIGHT! WOW! ISN'T THIS FUN?
BOY, I'LL SAY! NEW YEAR'S IS A **GAS!**

HEAVENS! I'M HAVING THE BEST TIME! WHAT DID YOU SAY YOUR NAME WAS?
MICHAEL DOONESBURY. HOW ABOUT YOU AND ME GOING OUT TO MY CAR?

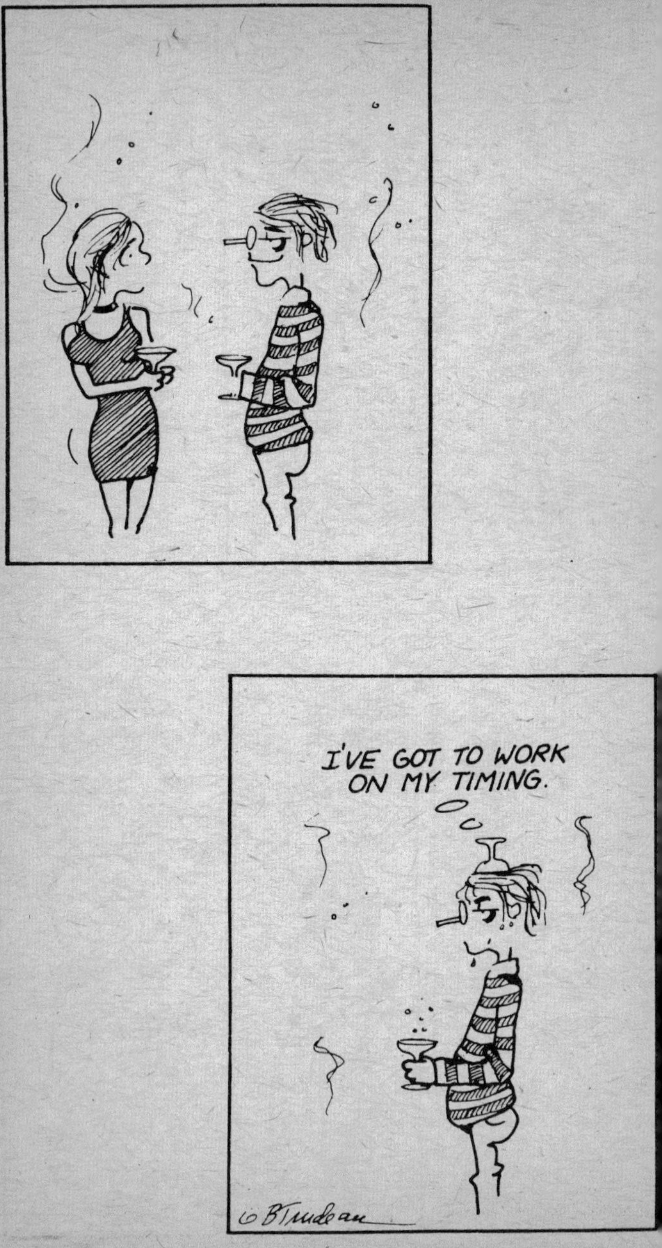
I'VE GOT TO WORK ON MY TIMING.
© BTrudeau

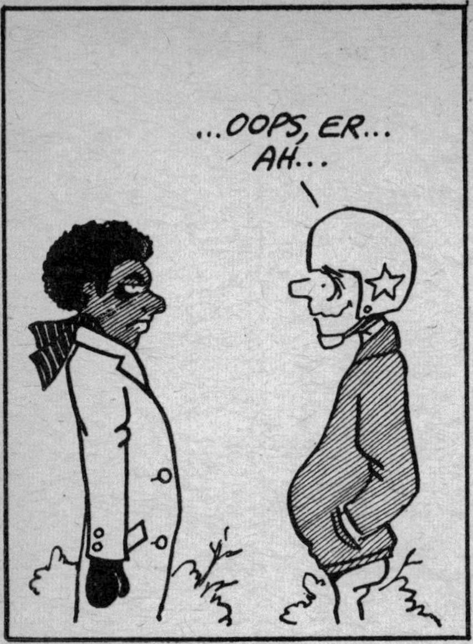
...OOPS, ER...
AH...

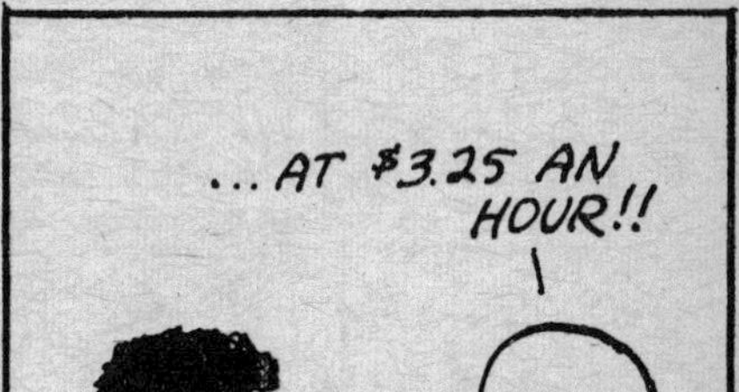
...AT $3.25 AN
HOUR!!
GBTrudeau

WELL, WE'RE IN THE AIR! ISN'T THIS EXCITING!
I'LL SAY! I JUST CAN'T WAIT TO GET TO WARM, SUNNY FORT LAUDERDALE.
THEN WHY ARE YOU ON THE FLIGHT TO CLEVELAND?

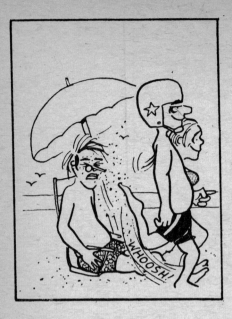

OH, MAN, WHEN THEY SEE THE HAVOC I'LL CAUSE, THE FUZZ WILL REGRET THE DAY THEY RELEASED ME FROM JAIL...
OF COURSE, THEY MAY ALREADY BE ON TO ME...
GBTrudeau